A New T.U.L.I.P.

A Kinder, Gentler Calvinism for the 21st Century

Keith M. Curran

A New T.U.L.I.P.: A Kinder, Gentler Calvinism for the 21st Century
ISBN: Softcover 978-1-955581-38-7
Copyright © 2021 by Keith M. Curran

All rights reserved. No part of this book may be reproduced or transmitted in any form or by any means, electronic or mechanical, including photocopying, recording, or by any information storage and retrieval system, without permission in writing from the publisher.

Parson's Porch Books is an imprint of Parson's Porch & Company (PP&C) in Cleveland, Tennessee. PP&C is an innovative organization which raises money by publishing books of noted authors, representing all genres. Its face and voice is **David Russell Tullock** (dtullock@parsonsporch.com).

Parson's Porch & Company *turns books into bread & milk* by sharing its profits with the poor.

www.parsonsporch.com

A New T.U.L.I.P.

Use, printing, permission and acknowledgements

This work is offered for the edification of the larger church. Individuals are encouraged to enjoy this work as a supplement to their spiritual growth. It can also be used for group study, a classroom resource or as a Church School discussion resource. There are many illustrations and stories included in the text that are perfect for sermon use. Those from non-Presbyterian or Reformed branches of the Faith will find this material interesting, edifying and informative, and will notice many commonalities with their own traditions. Each brief chapter includes a Scripture text for the reader to read prior to the chapter. So get your Bible or online Scripture app ready.

When quoting this project, please give appropriate credit to the author or quoted references.

The author has made a special effort to give appropriate credit to quoted sources and is appreciative for the ideas, stories, and good work of those who inspired this project. A tip of the hat is given to Brian McLaren for sparking the ideas behind this project. The brief paragraph on a new T.U.L.I.P. in <u>A Generous Orthodoxy</u>[1] was the springboard for this effort. His talks at the *Church Unbound Conference* at Montreat, NC in the summer of 2010 reinforced the material in this

---

[1] A Generous Orthodoxy, Brian McLaren, Zondervan, Grand Rapids, MI. 2005

work. McLaren indicated that the historic, mainline denominations, like the Presbyterian and Reformed Churches, offer a very accessible venue for 21st Century seekers. I hope the presentation in this book honors that opportunity to share the gospel in ways that make sense to post-modern people. I am also indebted to the late Ben Lacy Roses' small book on T.U.L.I.P.[2] His work is a great introduction to the topic for modern readers of all Faith traditions.

The phrase, a kinder, gentler Calvinism is a popular term these days and may have originated with Richard Mouw's book, *Calvinism and the Las Vegas Airport* (Zondervan, 2004). Others have used it freely and with different meanings. A quick Google search offers a few examples: William H. Smith, in The Aquila Report Newsletter, 7/5/2011, used this term in a book review of *Ten Myths About Calvinism: Recovering the Breadth of the Reformed Tradition* by Kenneth J. Stewart, IVP Academic. 2011. (https://theaquilareport.com/a-kinder-gentler-calvinism/) As well as Chris Meehan, in his blog for CRCN.org who used this term as a title on July 11, 2011. (https://www.crcna.org/news-and-events/news/kinder-gentler-john-calvin)

I thank the congregation of St. Andrew Presbyterian Church, Suffolk, VA, and the Massanetta Springs Bible Conference (2005) where these thoughts were fleshed out in sermon and lecture form. I would also like to thank my pastor in retirement, Rev. Dr. Steve Starzer, who encouraged me to

---

[2] TULIP: The Five Disputed Points of Calvinism, Ben Lacy Rose, Providence House Pub. 1996

publish this work. And also a big thank you goes to my wife, Debbie, for her lifelong encouragement and belief in me.

Scripture taken from *The Message*. Copyright- 1993, 1994, 1995, 1996, 2000, 2001, 2002. Used by permission of NavPress Publishing Group. Other Scripture quoted is from the website: www.biblegateway.com. Other scripture quoted is paraphrased by the author.

Introduction

"Theology matters" was a catch phrase a few seasons ago for Presbyterians (PCUSA). In light of conflicts in the church about spiritual practices, biblical interpretation, personal lifestyles, worship styles, and sexuality issues, the denomination at the time sought to find the root causes of such discord. It seems to all get back to theology; what we believe about God and how we understand those beliefs are being acted out in our lives. I share this work for the edification of the church and not to confront controversy or bolster a particular 'side' in ongoing theological matters.

As much as theology matters in how we deal with and understand the current issues of church and society, it is even more vital for the church today to be grounded in good theology for daily living and faith development. To know why we believe this or that, or to understand better what makes our faith tick, can deepen our convictions and better know ourselves in light of God's saving grace. Knowing the why or the what also helps us understand others in the church, whether it is a Presbyterian church or another denomination. In addition, knowing some basics about theology affords us some leverage when others ask us about our faith story or what we believe about God and godly things. By being better able to articulate one's own faith, makes contemporary Christians better evangelists especially when we approach the subject in a kinder and gentler fashion. Matthew 10:39 can serve as the theme text for kinder and gentler Calvinists in the

21st Century- *If your first concern is to look after yourself, you'll never find yourself. But if you forget about yourself and look to me, you'll find both yourself and me.*[3]

In this book, I've tried to condense a number of thoughts and insights that I've been struggling with as a minister in a society that is both Post-Modern and 'Post–Christian'. Serving an historic denomination has turned out to be a great vehicle for innovation as it allowed me to offer the church a broader way of doing theology that I believe makes sense in our contemporary life. After all, our Calvinistic roots provide a clarion call for theological innovation. The cry, *Reformed and always being reformed* has been the motto for Reformed Christians for over five centuries. I've used the late Ben Lacy Rose's very good contemporary view of T.U.L.I.P as a baseline for the series. His insights are priceless. Brian McLaren's brief mention of a kinder, gentler Calvinism in his book A Generous Orthodoxy serves as the outline for much of the content of the five newer ways to view T.U.L.I.P. He makes it easy to build on his brief musings. In fact, McLaren offers a challenge to denominations to take up his suggestions to update their theology for the 21st Century. I guess this is what I'm trying to do in this book.

My hope is that these brief chapters will catch your attention and pique your curiosity. By revisiting the old acrostic T.U.L.I.P. in our day, you and the church will appreciate not only our historic viewpoints but also be challenged to consider our faith and beliefs in new ways for a new day.

---

[3] The Message   Matt. 10:39

Theology really does matter for believers. I hope this brief work can help the larger church find this to be so.

Rev. Dr. Keith Curran, 2021

Chapter One

Read Psalm 49:1-9

Sadly, the historic Presbyterian denomination is being called by a different name of late. We used to be called one of the great 'mainline denominations' but now (even within church circles) we're being called one of the 'sideline denominations'. The denomination I am a part of has been shrinking since the mid-60s and only a handful of churches in each region are growing or holding their own. The church I served for 18 years, St. Andrew Church in Suffolk, VA, was blessed to be one of the growing congregations. Yet so many other local churches are pushing past Presbyterians in growth and influence. This is why there is a change in how society sees Presbyterians (and other historic mainline denominations) and it is sadly often quite accurate. Even though the congregation I served for many years has been blessed with a vitality and spirit that is contagious, it's still difficult at times for ministers, staff, church officers and members to express what they believe and why they think their church has something special to offer those seeking a church home and meaningful spiritual growth at this time. Can you succinctly say what you or your church believes and why that makes a mainline church like the Presbyterian or Reformed Church (or any other) a viable option for people today? That is not easy to do for any of us, including pastors and staff.

As we begin this journey of faith, I would like us to explore not only the traditional beliefs of the Reformed Faith, but also step out of our comfort zone, *thinking outside the box* (as my friend, Jim Shinn often advised before it became such a popular phrase), and discover a kinder, gentler theology for our day. The historic beliefs of the Reformed Faith have guided the church for hundreds of years but it is time to consider an alternative way of expressing that same historic faith in a way that better speaks to our age? I'm not saying that we should throw out the classic theology books and the historic confessions of the church and forget they ever existed. What I'm suggesting is that we find a new way to express the biblical truths that highlight the historic faith in new ways that address the foundational issues of our time. This book will take us by the hand and walk us through some new ways to express the gospel truth that resonates with today's issues and contemporary hearts, that is, if you let it. I hope you will.

The text from Psalm 49 can help us get started. One of the great insights of the Protestant Reformation is the realization that we, as it says in Ps. 49:7, <u>cannot</u> redeem ourselves. The traditional way of expressing our theology is to start with this truth and then see how that plays out. In like manner, we'll start with the historic insights of the Reformed Faith and then see how we can express these truths in ways that are better suited for contemporary ears and meet today's spiritual questions. After all, aren't we called to cast a line[4] into the neighborhood and our workplace and see if we can catch the

---

[4] Luke 5:10

attention of those who do not yet have an ongoing relationship with Christ and the church? Isn't it our holy task to engage with those who have disengaged from the local church and try to lure them back into the fellowship of faith? You are invited to go on a journey of faith that will not only inform you of the historic T.U.L.I.P. acrostic of Reformed Theology but also be introduced to a new way to express our faith in kinder and gentler ways in the 21st Century. So, as I like to do most days, let's go fishing, but not for bass, but for those whom God is calling us to befriend[5] in Jesus' name. We're about to take off on an adventure in faith.

Prayer: Lord of every address on my street, may your Spirit inspire me and my church to find a way to interest those who have yet to invite you into their lives. May I be a part of that for the sake of your Kingdom. Amen.

Notes:

---

[5] II Cor. 5:17-19   See the Good News Bible for a great contemporary rendering of being a friendmaker for God.

Chapter Two

T.U.L.I.P. A Kinder, Gentler Calvinism for the 21st Century

Triune Love, Unselfish Election, Limitless Reconciliation, Inspiring Grace, and Passionate, Persistent Saints

Read Psalm 63:1-8

It's long, but not the longest title ever. I came across a children's book with a world record title:

<u>Red Ranger</u>: The story of a boy and his dog, an Alaskan Husky, who battle the brutal winter of the Northwest Territory and find solace in their friendship amidst the background of the last gold rush in Canada which attracted some of the era's meanest and grizzliest characters who come face to face with the boy and his dog, Red Ranger; the smartest, three-legged dog with a heart of pure Canadian gold.

With a title like that I don't think it's necessary to read the book! Maybe with a title like this one it's not necessary to read my book, but I hope you will. Each chapter is chock full of good, grace-filled theology and isn't that something the church needs *more* of these days?

First, are you familiar with the acrostic T.U.L.I.P. that lists the five traditional points of Calvinism (Reformed/Presbyterian theology)? In general, it seems to be a generational response. Those with scores of candles on a birthday cake are more likely to know what T.U.L.I.P. is, or at least know something about it. One Sunday in church, I asked this question of the almost 300 in worship and only 3 people raised their hands. T.U.L.I.P. is a relic from the old school, but I think it's a valuable one worth resurrecting for the 21st Century, although in a kinder, gentler format.

Can you remember what it means?[6]

> T:
> U:
> L:
> I:
> P:

The theology of our Presbyterian/Reformed heritage is based on the monumental work of John Calvin who lived in the 16th Century and along with Luther and other Reformers brought in the Protestant Reformation and a new world order. Calvin's teachings have guided the Protestant church for 500 years. Those 16th and early 17th Century revolutionary teachings transformed the Western world and rejuvenated the Christian faith of the Middle Ages. Calvin and others addressed their teachings to their age, bringing clarity and spiritual assurance to the masses. They sought to confront the errors they saw in the Church as it was emerging from the Middle Ages. The Reformers challenged the current beliefs

---

[6] Try Googling it.

and theology and tried to provide new answers to the questions that lay at the heart of those who sought a more biblical perspective on the Christian life and beliefs. The Reformation blossomed and flourished in Europe and Britain. The Church was transformed and revival spread to the New World. Pilgrims brought Reformed beliefs to Massachusetts, the Dutch Reformed landed in New York and the Scotch Irish Presbyterians colonized the Middle Colonies.

It was within this cultural and religious context, that the acrostic T.U.L.I.P helped generations of Christians understand the main points of Reformed theology. This teaching tool taught children and adults the basics of Calvin's teachings. These words of assurance and acceptance, gave believers a sure and certain hope of forgiveness in this life and a home with God in the next.

Yet over time, in some circles, Calvinism became a strict and often graceless expression of the gospel. It was a theology, when read in its strictest interpretation, excluded many and painted a picture of the spiritual life as icy cold, fatalistic and judgmental.

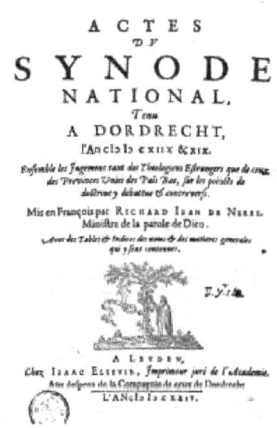

The Dutch Reformed Church (thus the tulip symbol) at the Council of Dort (1618-19) coined the acrostic that has been used to teach basic Reformed Theology for generations. But because of the determinism inherent in this theological viewpoint, many Christians, in good conscience, (declared a scruple or concern) and could not go along with part or all of it and at times, bloody battles erupted over Calvinistic claims. Arminianism vs. Calvinism became a long-standing *'us against them'* feud lingering even into our day. Vestiges of the battle can be seen as you drive by the local Baptist churches. The traditional Baptist Church is Calvinistic but down the street you'll see a sign for a Free Will Baptist Church, which radically disputes Calvinistic predestination claims[7].

A Free Will Baptist minister was waking down the street with a traditional Baptist minister discussing predestination. The traditional Baptist minister tripped on the curb and fell down, tearing his good pants and scrapping his knee. The Free Will Baptist minister said, "I suppose God planned that fall before the foundations of the earth and knew that was going to happen today." "Yes" said the traditional Baptist, "and I'm glad that's over with!"

---

[7] Predestination is often understood as something being pre-planned by a divine source.

Have you ever been able to understand predestination? It's a very difficult concept to grasp. Some just ignore it, yet there it is in the Bible. I often say that predestination is the one doctrine that must be seen from behind. It's only when we look back over our lives that we see God's hand guiding our lives in ways that accomplished God's will. Can you think of a time when God was guiding you but at the time you didn't realize it? Jot it down here if you like.

Prayer: Lord of all time and dimensions; thank you for guiding me and leading me even though at the time I did not realize it. Forgive me for thinking that I'm always in total control. Let me remember that you're at work in me even when I do not see it in the moment. Amen.

Notes:

Chapter Three

Read John 3:16-17

A link in *Presbyterian Outlook* to an article in the Baptist Press News caught my eye. **T.U.L.I.P.: Divine sovereignty, human responsibility**.[8] In it Prof. Daniel Akin, president of Southeastern Baptist Seminary in NC explains the T.U.L.I.P. acrostic to a denomination that often doesn't even realize it is Calvinistic in theology. He does a good job on the five points but pauses for a longer look when it comes to free will vs. election. That's still a hot button issue for lots of Christians, not just Southern Baptists. Akin quotes the great Baptist evangelist, Charles Spurgeon (who called himself a 5 Point Calvinist…sic T.U.L.I.P.) and his ability to juxtapose predestination with his matchless evangelistic fervor. The article reads:

"That God predestines and persons are responsible, are two things that few can see. Two truths cannot be contradictory to each other. These two truths…are two lines that are so nearly parallel, that the mind that shall pursue them farthest, will never discover that they converge; but they do converge, and they will meet somewhere in eternity, close to the throne of God, whence all truth doth spring. Both are true; no two truths can be inconsistent with each other, and what you have to do is to believe them both." [9]

---

[8] Presbyterian Outlook, Daniel Akin, www.bpnews.net   Apr. 4, 2006
[9] Ibid pg. 4

I'm glad the Baptists are thinking theologically, aren't you? They challenge the rest of us to do more if it.

Presbyterians today are still painted with the broad brush of Calvinism even though we've left behind strict adherence to the T.U.L.I.P doctrines. When I was a serving pastor I was asked at least monthly if we still believe in double predestination. (For those who don't know what that is, it's a logical outcome of believing that if some are predested to be saved for heaven, then others must be predestined to go to hell. Not a very flattering consequence of grace, is it?) Back in the 90's, a retired Union Presbyterian Seminary (Richmond) professor wrote a little book that tried to make the 5 disputed points of Calvinism more acceptable and applicable to the modern church. The late Ben Lacy Rose did a great job of it. [10] He'll be our guide as we refresh our understanding of the traditional way of looking at T.U.L.I.P. First, we'll take a look at the traditional T.U.L.I.P. before we consider an updated, *kinder, gentler version for the 21st Century.*[11] This is a good time to read Romans 7:18-24.

T: Total Depravity- Human nature has been and is utterly corrupted by sin so that no one is capable of doing anything to <u>accomplish one's own salvation</u>. All life is tainted by sin, even our best efforts. Even our deepest love, even the noblest sacrifice, cannot escape being somewhat, in some unconscious way self-centered. Romans 7:18-24 points this

---

[10] TULIP: The Five Disputed Points of Calvinism, Ben Lacy Rose, Providence House Pub. 1996
[11] I believe this term originated in Richard Mouw's book, "Calvinism and the Las Vegas Airport."

out. Thus, no one can claim that a life is so good and well lived that they don't need God to save them. Professor Mark Achtemeier said at a church conference, *"Properly understood, this doctrine is not quite so pessimistic, but it does bear the disconcerting reminder that no area of human life is immune from the distorting effects of sin. Humans, as fallen creatures, have this tendency to lapse into sin even in the course of our best deeds and most noble intentions."*[12]

It's easy to see why this raises lots of questions. Many misread it and only hear that people are cursed with evil and malice and there is no good in anyone. Others believe evil is a choice and not a condition of the human soul, believing that people are innocent until an actual sin is committed.

Do you agree that even our best efforts, our most sincere love and acts of kindness are tainted by self-centeredness (even just a little bit) or a hope for some sort of pay off? I think this is what the T is trying to teach us.

Prayer: Lord, in my love, kindness, and care, let me offer them with a gracious heart even though there may be within me a hint of ego or reward. Let me do it anyway. Amen.

Notes:

---

[12] The Layman Online, July 10, 2006

Chapter Four

Read John 6:37-47

U-Unconditional Election- God has chosen a people for the sake of God's purposes in the world. Faith is a gift that is freely bestowed upon us. So it was God who began a good work of faith in you before you made any conscious choice about it. God chose you before you chose to follow God. Ephesians 2:8 says that it's by God's grace we've been saved and not as a result of our own efforts so that we can do the good things God has already planned for us. John 6:37-47 may also apply here. Thus, no one can claim that they 'found God' but only that God found them. *"I was lost but now I am found...."* It takes someone to <u>find</u> the lost such as a shepherd finding a lost lamb. That 'Someone' is God. When someone says that 'they came to Christ', what really was happening is that Christ came to them, a seeking soul.

Yet, if some are chosen, then others are left out of the grace of God. Are some people actually predestined to go to hell? Would a loving God do that? Do you think this is what this means? If not, can you think of why God would choose some and why? Consider Israel, the chosen nation. Why didn't God choose Rome or China or the Congo? Wouldn't Greece, Egypt or England have been a better choice to spread the gospel?

Limited Atonement- The traditional view of atonement is that the work of the cross is available to the whole world, yet it is valid only for those who believe it to be true and then confess or claim it. Thus it is *limited* to those who accept the gift of salvation. To enjoy a birthday present, you must accept it from the giver and open it to enjoy it. In much the same way, the grace of God and salvation must be accepted to be enjoyed. John 17:6-9 talks of this. Jesus knew that not everyone who heard the gospel would believe and receive his grace. That must have frustrated the Lord.

Questions arise. Was the cross only for those whom God knew beforehand would believe and accept its grace? What about God loving the whole *world* in John 3:16 or Jesus being the Lamb of God who takes away the sin of the *world*? Does that mean that those who never heard about Jesus or are incapable of making a verbal profession of faith or our Jewish cousins or the spiritually faithful of other religions are locked out of heaven? Peppering the church with *these* questions can turn even the brightest Christian into a babbling idiot or worse, seem like a religious bigot.

Maybe it is time to talk about the atonement using different words and symbols. Can you think of another way of putting it? Can you come up with other biblical images that express the gracious love of God for his people? Jot down your thoughts here.

Prayer: *Thank you for the gift of salvation and even more, thank you for making it real for me so that I can accept the truth of it. Now let me live it out in ways that bring honor to you. Amen.*

Notes:

Chapter Five

Read Ephesians 2:10

I **Irresistible Grace**- Our salvation from beginning to end is the work of God alone. God's grace was at work before we believed, it allowed us to believe, and keeps us believing. The clay, which the potter works, cannot resist what the potter's hands create. Ephesians 2:10 says, *"God has made us what we are."* God is at work in you, molding you into a disciple, God's person in the world. Which means often we are surprised to see God at work in our humble lives, doing God's will and fulfilling God's purposes. There are a lot of Steve Urkles in the church. We stumble into doing God's will and we hear ourselves say, *"Did I do that?"*

But some wonder that if God's pull is 'simply irresistible', then do we really have free will, a choice in the matter? (Remember the Free Will Baptists? This is their question.) Where does free will and choice come into play in salvation? What about Joshua back in Old Testament days who claimed that he and his family were going to choose God rather than worship Baal?

Do we have a choice in the matter? Is it all up to us? If God is all-powerful, then can't God do anything, even save everyone? When the good news of Jesus was set before you, did you feel like it was your choice to believe it? How was the Spirit working behind the scenes in your life at that time?

P **Perseverance of the Saints**- Perseverance : *persistence in doing something despite difficulty or delay in achieving success.*[13] Once God has begun a good work in you; God will see it through to the end.[14] There is a blessed assurance for those who are heirs to salvation. God never takes back the gift of grace. Thus, in humbleness, we can know for certain that we are God's people of faith; we are children of God. The hope cannot be taken away. The phrase, 'once saved, always saved' sounds like a Baptist saying, but in fact it's a way to verbalize the doctrine of the Perseverance of the Saints. James Ayers, in a column in <u>Presbyterians Today,</u> answers a reader's question about 'once saved, always saved" by indicating that it's not as simple as that. He says Scripture states that God will hold on to us (John 10:27-29, Romans 8:35-39) but also it's our responsibility to hold on to God and persevere (see Hebrews10:36-39).[15]

But, someone may counter, what about the church member who is a scoundrel or church folks who fall away from the church and never come back? Does that mean they never really were believers in the first place? (But remember... unconditional election.) Professor Rose explains the doctrine using the illustration of a sailor in a storm. He is knocked down on the deck of the ship but is never thrown overboard.

---

[13] AOL.COM search
[14] Phil. 1:6
[15] Presbyterians Today, June/July 2006. pg. 38

God never deserts us even when we fall away from the church. But is this the reality for everyone who turns his or her back on God? I think it's a legitimate question.

Prayer: *Lord, I pray for those who have turned their backs on you; those who have fallen away from the church. I pray for those in my family who used to be faithful but now act like faith is unimportant and church is a bore. Bless them with a renewed spirit and a recharged faith. Bring them back into the fold once more. Amen.*

Notes:

Chapter Six

Read Exodus 20:1-17

Although I believe the 5 points are theologically valid and Scriptural, (after all I'm a red-blooded Presbyterian) I think it may be time to highlight a timelier set of Presbyterian beliefs for a 21st Century world using the acrostic T.U.L.I.P. but encouraging a kinder, gentler Calvinism. But some might argue that we don't need a new list, the old is just fine as it is. In fact, that's exactly what a visitor to worship yelled across the narthex as he went out the door after a sermon on a new T.U.L.I.P. It was fortunate that I served a church where things like that didn't happen very often. The young man, about 30, visited our church on the first day of the sermon series on how the church can offer a kinder, gentler Calvinism, and heard me list the traditional doctrines like I'm doing here and promise that the next Sunday I'd be suggesting a

Photo by author

kinder, gentler T.U.L.I.P. for the 21st Century. At the door we shook hands and I asked his name. Then, as he made it to the doors, the visitor yelled back, *"**We don't need a new***

T.U.L.I.P. The old one is just fine as it is." He didn't return to hear my ideas. So I ask, "Is it time for a more grace-filled theology that speaks to the needs of today's situations or should we leave well enough alone?"

That's the question I was wrestling with when I saw the *Weekly World News* in the grocery store checkout line. "10 More Commandments Found!" the headline blared. It seems Moses got so mad he threw down the stone tables. But he only got to read those on the front side. According to the article, no one realized there were 10 more on the back until the original tables were found recently and pieced back together. My old biblical archeology professor, Charles Fritsch would have loved to get his hands on those newly discovered tables.

The additional 10 read:

11 Thou shalt tolerate the faith of others, as you would have them do unto you.
12 In matters of business thou shalt protect the rights of laborers, as Pharaoh should have done.
13 Thou shalt not put thy animals' rights before people, either in body or in spirit.
14 Thou shalt not inhale burning leaves in a house of manna where it may affect the breathing of others.
15 Thou shalt remit a portion of thy worldly goods to be collected by agents of the ruling party.
16 Thou shalt not elect a fool to lead thee. If twice elected, thy punishment shall be death by stoning.

17 Thou shalt not cry 'fire and brimstone' in a large public gathering.

18 Thou shalt not erect a temple of gambling in the desert, where all will become wanton.

19 They body is sacred and thou shalt not permanently alter thy face or bosom. If thy nose offends thee,
leave it alone.

And only a fragment of the 20th was found that left it uninterpretable. Only the words 'thou *shalt not*' and the words '*war*' *and 'oil' being readable.* [16]

Although I don't think we need to update the Decalogue for the 21st Century, I am open to investigating a kinder, gentler T.U.L.I.P. for the church of our day.

Kinder and gentler; do I think the traditional T.U.L.I.P. is too harsh? It is in some circles. An extreme illustration: The Westboro Baptist Church. You know the church from news reports of the pastor and church members protesting at the funerals of soldiers killed in the War Against Terroism. Their claim is that the war and the casualties are due to God's punishment of the USA for being open to gay rights. Their church web site is www.godhatesfags.com. They declare; "*We are a T.U.L.I.P. Baptist Church! We believe and vigorously preach-the 5 Points of Calvinism! Anyone preaching otherwise is a Hell-bound false prophet, a messenger of Satan. Let him be accursed of God!*"[17] With

---

[16] Weekly World News, June 27, 2005. pg. 24-25
[17] www.godhatesfags.com

churches using T.U.L.I.P. as hate speech, I hope it's not too late for a kinder, gentler Calvinism for the 21st Century.

Emergent Church leader, Brian McLaren shared this sentiment in his book, *A Generous Orthodoxy*. In it he proposes a T.U.L.I.P. that may produce a kinder, gentler Calvinism[18] to help answer the faith questions and concerns of people today. In a brief few paragraphs he challenges many denominations to rethink their theology to better answer today's questions. McLaren challenges Presbyterian and Reformed churches to consider an updated T.U.L.I.P. This work will build on his updated acrostic and flesh out what it can mean for the church and contemporary Presbyterians, as well as all Christians.

Can you think of other examples of when the church or a particular congregation has been exclusive, hateful, selfish, or violent? Why do you think people follow such teachings even though they know that Jesus would never have taught such things? What is it that lets human beings turn off their rational thinking and tune into something so harmful?

Prayer: Lord, forgive your church when it strays from the path of Jesus' teachings. Forgive me when I stray. Amen.

Notes:

---

[18] A Generous Orthodoxy, Brian McLaren, Zondervan, 2005 pg. 195

Chapter Seven

Read Psalm 8

T

Triune Love_ A kinder, gentler Calvinism would say that the T stands for Triune Love.

Brian McLaren wrote that blindly sticking to distinctive denominational doctrines in our day and age is a lot like cigarettes. The use of which often leads to a hard-to-break Protestant habit that is hazardous to spiritual health (and that makes the breath smell bad).[19] I'd hate to have folks at my church repel seekers because of bad breath or doctrines designed to answer questions of those who lived generations long ago. I think it may be time that we offer a kindler, gentler Calvinism for the 21st Century.

Our Reformed Faith, based on the theology of Protestant Reformer John Calvin in the 16th Century and those who came after him, has good news to share that makes good sense for our day and age even though we may need to highlight different aspects of it now that we're living in the 21st Century.

---

[19] Brian McLaren, Generous Orthodoxy, pg. 195

The motto of Reformed Theology is that we are *Reformed and Always Being Reformed according to the Word of God.* My denomination, Presbyterians, are a branch of the Protestant Church that strives to present the gospel to the world in ways that answer contemporary questions that may be very different from those that were asked in generations past.

Back in Protestant Holland in the time of the Council of Dort some 400 years ago, the questions of the day challenged the church to reinforce particular Scriptural beliefs such as: no one is good enough to make it to heaven on their own merits. A person could not work, buy, or be holy enough to earn their own salvation. They were assured that before the foundation of the world, God had chosen a people to do God's will on earth. They were taught that the divine gift of the cross has to be accepted for it to be effective. That it is God who saves us and we can't take any credit for our salvation. And that God will not abandon believers even though some may end up turning their backs on God or being kicked out of the church (excommunicated) because of their Protestant beliefs.

These were core issues at the time of the Reformation and had to be clarified. But what about *our* questions of faith today? Does the church have answers that connect to the issues and attitudes of todays confused, conflicted, crowded, yet isolated world? I like to think so.

So I'd like to suggest that we use that old Calvinist acrostic, T.U.L.I.P. and give it a bit of a twist and turn to make it into a teaching tool that helps answer today's issues of faith and life.

Originally we heard that the T stood for Total Depravity (a nice upbeat thought). That means that people are like Ivory Soap: even our best efforts and deepest love is at best, only 99 and 47/100% pure. No one is perfect! But do we always have to emphasize the negative? A kinder, gentler Calvinism could say that the T stands for **TRIUNE LOVE**. What I mean by this is that we can know and sense and experience and pray with an expectation that God's love will be shown to us in ways that are expressed in Trinitarian fashion. We believe in one God and that God is known to us as Father, Son and Divine Spirit or put another way: Creator, Redeemer, and divine Presence.

We can know and sense and experience and pray for God's love to be shown to us in ways that are expressed in Trinitarian fashion. A recent PCUSA 'Trinity Paper'[20] was designed to help the church find ways to understand and be more expressive in worshiping our Triune God. Knowing that God; Father, Son and Spirit, loves the world and can be known by every human being on earth no matter what denomination, religious affiliation or philosophical school of thought is key. Creation is designed to express the good news to all people.

The other morning I woke up early. The dog demanded I take him for a walk. The sun was just coming up. Looking east, a line of puffy clouds stretched across the horizon as if it

---

[20] http://www.pcusa.org/media/uploads/theologyandworship/pdfs/migliore.pdf

had been drawn using a ruler. I learned long ago from an old dairy farmer that clouds like that were called a 'buttermilk sky' and it forecasts rain. Dramatic reddish clouds sat below the white streams of cotton. 'Red sky in morning, sailor take warning' goes the old wisdom I learned from my father. But it wasn't just a light pink sky. Brushed across the puffs of cloud were blazing orange, red, and deep pink like the glow of a brush fire seen from a distance. It was a spooky kind of beautiful. The 'take your breath away' kind of moment that David Letterman would call an 'Extravaganza!" And it was. In the few passing moments of the haunting blaze of fiery sky I kept hearing 'Sailor take warning'. A storm's due. Trouble's coming.

Then, without even knowing I needed a good word, I heard the Creator whisper a familiar refrain: *My steadfast love endures forever.*[21] The moment of unease I sensed taking in the threatening sky disappeared. The Creator of all that is seen and unseen, said that I'm loved with a love that will not let me go: storm or no storm!

God the Creator is forever sending signs our way, and whispering to our souls: *My steadfast love endures forever. You are loved with a love that will never let you go.* What's that mean to you?

The Apostle John wrote to the early Christian community saying that God is love.[22] When you look at that passage today, it's easy to miss the Trinitarian terminology that John

---

[21] See Psalm 136
[22] I John 4:8

used. God loves us and we know that because he gave us his only Son to be our salvation. We know that's true because we know God's presence (the Spirit) in our lives. And we know that's true because we can love one another as Christians.

> "The person who refuses to love doesn't know the first thing about God, because God is love—so you can't know him if you

Triune Love is the "Primal Essence of God" says McLaren.[23] It's the prime cause and the divine conclusion. It's Emmanuel (God with us). It's redemption. It is Jesus himself offering a love that will not let you go.

Triune Love is divine love experienced in ways that express the love of God; Creator, Redeemer, Presence. It's the love we feel when we sense the **Presence of God**. And that can be experienced by anyone.

Back in the 1920's Harvey Penick bought a red spiral notebook and started to jot down his thoughts on the game of golf. Over the years the notebook filled up with his observations and insights. He never showed it to anyone except his son. Then, in 1991 he showed his red notebook to a local writer who suggested he think about getting it published. A call came to the house from Simon and Schuster that they wanted to publish his book and told Harvey's wife that the advance would be $90,000.

---

[23] Brian McLaren, Generous Orthodoxy, pg. 195

When Harvey Penick, now up in years, heard this, his heart sank. His family didn't understand why he was so down. Then he explained. With all the medical bills he had, he couldn't afford to advance the publisher that much money to get the book in print. His writer friend had to explain that it was the publisher that was going to pay him $90,000 for the book. The book, <u>Harvey Penick's Little Red Book</u>, went on to sell over a million copies. [24]

People often have a Harvey Penick's reaction to the extravagant offer of God's love in Jesus Christ. We say, "I can't afford that! Or 'what do I have to do?'" And Jesus says, "*Nothing. It's already been paid in full. Just take the grace, it's a gift and enjoy your life.*"

Triune Love is the Primal Essence of God.[25] It's the prime cause and the divine conclusion. It's Emmanuel. It's redemption. It is **Jesus** himself offering a love that will not let you go. Triune Love is divine love experienced in ways that express the love of God: the Father, the Son, and the Holy Spirit. It's the love we feel when we sense the **Presence of God**. Often it's hard to describe and even harder to figure out.

It's a little thing here, a coincidence there.
It's a perfect moment, or a lesson learned the hard way.
A loss, a gain, a missed opportunity.

---

[24] Eric Hulstrand at http://elbourne.org/sermons/index.mv?illustration+4764
[25] Brian McLaren, Generous Orthodoxy, pg. 195

It's an ironic situation and a clarifying thought.
It's serendipity and disappointment.
It's pain and frustration and exhilaration.
It could even be boredom or a flash of enlightenment.
It's a little of this and a lot of that.
It's the Spirit of God...
Soft as a whisper, warm as a breeze,
Comforting as a long embrace.[26]

When we experience the love of God's Presence, often it's like making biscuits. The flour itself is bland, the baking powder doesn't taste good and neither does the salt or Crisco. But when put together by a loving mom or dad, they come out just right.

Often life at times is bland, sour, tasteless or too sharp, but the Spirit of God takes the ingredients and mixes them up and bakes them and then, to our surprise, things come out just right. Why does that happen? It happens because of an ancient promise that's still at the core of God's Triune Essence: *My steadfast love endures forever.* In other words, you are loved with a love that will never let you go.

Prayer: In the name of the Father, the Son and the Holy Spirit, our Triune God. Amen.

---

[26] *I can't remember if I wrote this myself or heard it somewhere and used it in a sermon sometime. Sorry that I can't recall a source or when I wrote it.*

Chapter Eight

Read Matthew 10:39

U

Unselfish Election. Brian McLaren observes a troubling phenomenon. People are treating the church as a purveyor of religious goods and services. People are shopping for the best deals. [27] People are hopping from steeple to steeple in hopes of having their spiritual needs and emotional desires met. And the church is buying into the mentality of the church shopper. But, he reminds us, "**Christians aren't the end users of the gospel**".[28] The gospel isn't just about my salvation or yours; my happiness or yours. It doesn't end there. In fact, this is where it all begins.

T.U.L.I.P. may be partly to blame for this. If we say the U only stands for Unconditional Election- this means before the foundations of the world, God chose a people to receive blessings and being blessed by God become the sole focus of those who are blessed? Back at a time when the Church and bishops decided who was in and who was out of God's favor, such a word of assurance was a welcome relief. God chose *those* who would be blessed, not the church. That was good

---
[27] A Generous Orthodoxy, Pg. 107
[28] Pg. 107

news. But over time, a theological belief that was a great help to so many believers started to be misunderstood and misrepresented. Theologian Leslie Newbigin claimed that the most stubborn heresy in the history of monotheism is the belief that God chooses people for exclusive privilege.[29] If some are chosen, then can't it be argued that others are not? And what's that mean for those who are chosen? Faith can easily resort to the attitude, "It's all about me" or "I'm in and you're not."

But what happens if we start to understand that **Christians aren't the end users of the gospel.** *That it's not all about me, but for the sake of thee.* God chose us, not so we can have elite privileges or claims of specialness. Instead, a kinder, gentler Calvinism would see election (chosen-ness) as a gift that is given to some for the benefit of all others. To be chosen means we're blessed to be a blessing, healed to heal, enriched to enrich society, and taught to teach our family. An unselfish election, says McLaren, would be a reformation in Reformed Theology and it would be liberating![30] And the mission for the church would be to invite others into the family of faith so that they too can be blessed and then go on to be a blessing to others. God so loved the whole world that he sent his Son, not to condemn the world but to redeem it.[31] The showers of blessings would ready us to be a church that would bless others across the world. Unselfish Election is a gift that is given to some for the benefit of all others in hopes

---

[29] Pg. 195
[30] Pg. 196
[31] John 3:16-17 author's paraphrase

that all others will be included in the blessings. And the possibilities are unlimited!

There's an old legend that the carpenter Jesus made the best oxen yokes in all of the Galilee. People from all over the countryside came to Jesus for custom-fitted yokes for their work animals. In those days, as now, craftsman displayed their specialty above the door as a sign. It was said that Jesus' carpenter shop had a yoke displayed above the door and the words: MY YOKES FIT WELL

This is just a legend, but the point of the story is clear. The life Jesus chose for us before the foundations of the earth is not a life of privilege or special treatment, but it's also not a burden designed to weigh us down with meaningless dos and don'ts, guilt and shame. Jesus himself custom fits each believer for a life of service with a yoke that fits well. He said, *"My yoke is easy and the load I chose you to carry for me is light."* [32]

One of the key points I tried to instill in those taking on leadership in the churches I served was the oxymoron 'servant leadership'. It does sound like a contradiction in terms but in fact it a biblical principle of leadership. It means that those chosen for leadership in the church are to express that blessing in an attitude of servanthood. The symbol of this is the basin and towel based on the gospel story of when Jesus washed the feet and hands of his disciples. Readying to eat supper, Jesus took off his tunic and picked up a basin and towel to fulfill the Jewish cleanliness code prescribed in

---

[32] Matt. 11:30

Scripture. When entering a home, the host was to wash the feet and hands of visitors before eating. By the time of the Gospels, this task was usually delegated to a household servant. Seeing it wasn't done, Jesus took on the lowly task. As was his custom, Jesus used this simple household ritual as a teachable moment. You may remember his disciples put up a fight, protesting that they should be washing Jesus' feet. They were embarrassed that their leader would take on the role of a servant. Jesus demonstrated an attitude shift by showing them that if they were to be in leadership in the church, they had to do so in the spirit of a servant…counting others more important then self.[33]

Yet this attitude goes counter to our cultural norms, doesn't it? Who usually gets the attention, who gets the first crack at the office donuts? Who gets the executive rest room or the company car? It's the boss or supervisor or pastor or elder. This is the radical nature of leadership in the church. We're chosen not to lord it over others, but to be in an attitude of servanthood for the sake of Christ.

A funny thing happened on the way to communion. Sounds like the beginning of a preacher joke, but it really happened and it is a real-life lesson of servant leadership. I served as an Army Chaplain in the National Guard. One time on annual training, our Headquarters Company was set up out in the woods for field training. It was a Sunday morning and I arranged to have communion for the company. I set up my Chaplain's kit on the hood of a Jeep. Yes, just like those

---

[33] See Gen. 18:4 and John 13:3-5, 14

pictures you see in the movies. Folding chairs were arranged in a semi-circle and I played church songs on a boom box. Worshipers gathered and took their seats.

Now, before I go on, I have to explain that our commanding officer was a Colonel about to be promoted to General. (This was a huge honor for our command.) He was also a Presbyterian elder back at his local church. He agreed to serve the bread while I served the cup. For Presbyterians, it's an honor and responsibility for church elders to serve communion with the pastor, so he was happy to do it.

After a brief sermon I invited our commanding officer to come up so that we could serve the company communion. I explained the procedure that we would be serving each the bread and cup in an act of servanthood, counting others more important than self. What I didn't expect was the reaction to having the commanding officer, almost a general, serving the privates and corporals in the unit. Most were not churched and had little experience with worship so they were puzzled by the fact that the 'almost' general was serving the privates. Shouldn't it be the other way around? I once heard a comedian joke about the Army way…wondering what's more private than a general and what's more general than a private. This was at play on this occasion. Hesitancy kept many from moving forward for communion. Then, slowly the worshipers around this make-shift chancel made their way to us. Our commanding officer, an experienced elder, said, "The body of Christ broken for you". It was a bit of a shock for most, but what a lesson of servant leadership. We are chosen to be a blessing to others.

Can it be that a more challenging gospel for the 21st Century affirms the biblical truth that we are chosen by God before the foundations of the earth, not just to be blessed with grace and salvation, but to be a source of blessings to all others? I think a lot more people will give a listen to the gospel when it's put this way because people genuinely want to make a difference in the world. The showers of blessings ready us to be a church that will bless others in the world. Unselfish Election is a gift that is given to some for the benefit of all others in hopes that they too will join the blessed family of faith. Isn't this a great way to understand this blessing?

Lt. Col. Barb Sherer had to go through dozens of rigorous trials and required steps to be where she is today. She is a Presbyterian chaplain in the Army. She was chosen to serve in the armed forces after being chosen to serve as a minister in the denomination and before that she was selected for seminary training and prior to that the elders of her local church approved her pursuit of a call to ministry. She went up the ranks from Lieutenant to Lieutenant Colonel and was selected to go into Iraq, a war zone to minister to soldiers and the local Iraqis. She has been chosen many times in the span of her life, and some of those choices were completely out of her control. In response, Chaplain Sherer, has chosen to be a source of blessing to others.

"Hey, chaplain, will you bless my Humvee?" She said she normally didn't bless things, but she thought it couldn't hurt. They gathered around the vehicle and she prayed, *"Lord, bless this vehicle. Bless its driver; keep him alert and awake and able to face difficult situations. And bring him safely home."*

When she saw the impact the blessing had on the troops, she offered to bless all the vehicles in the unit, over 100 of them. She wasn't prepared for what happened next as she went from truck to truck. She saw one driver starting at her intently, even though a sandstorm had come up, and through the windshield she saw the driver mouth, 'Thank you." Then she got it. It wasn't some touchy, feely thing. It was a reminder of God's presence and protection. Later, she stood by her own Humvee as a soldier walked up, put a hand on the hood and closed his eyes for a few moments. He said he'd seen her blessing everyone else vehicle and he wanted to pray for hers. In that moment she knew she would never see a blessing in the same way again.[34]

The chaplain had been chosen, going through many rigorous steps so that she in turn could be a source of blessing to all others. Unselfish Election at work! Wow!

Prayer: Lord, thank you for the many stories of your will at work in our lives. Bless those who serve as chaplains and those who are called to ministry. Bless those who volunteer at church and in ministries across our community. Bless all who call you Lord. Amen.

---

[34] Presbyterians Today, Oct. 2004 pg. 10

Notes:

Chapter Nine

Read 2 Cor. 5:19-20

L

Limitless Reconciliation_ I'm suggesting that the L stand for **Limitless Reconciliation**. Or another way of putting it is to say it's about a *70 x 7 attitude*.

In Reformation times, the L- stood for Limited Atonement, and it meant that the work of the cross of Jesus Christ was limited only to those who truly believe it to be for them and understand the cross' implications on faith and life and eternity. By emphasizing the limited nature of salvation, it is natural to have many questions about those who are not believers. But what happens when we emphasize what is unlimited in the gospel? Can it catch the ear of those who criticize the church for only being concerned about who's making it to heaven and who is going to hell? Caring about the lost is paramount, but can we share the unlimited nature

> Paul says, "We beg you, let God change you."

of the gospel with our neighbors, coworkers, dorm-mates and teammates in hopes that they might find in a faith like ours a place where they can sense the limitless grace and genuine Triune love of God for them?

What comes in unlimited quantities in the gospel? **Reconciliation**. The Apostle Paul said it best to the Corinthian Church some 2000 years ago; *"When anyone is joined to Christ, she or he is a new creation; the old is gone, and the new has come. All this is done by God, who through Christ changed us from enemies into God's friends and gave us the task of making others God's friends as well."* (2 Cor.5:17-18)[35]

Paul goes on to say that the task we have been given is to share with as many as possible that God is trying to make everyone God's friends by not keeping an account of their sin but offering a fresh start. And then Paul says, "We beg you, let God change you." [36]

Two brothers were arguing over a checkers match. One demanded that when his checker reached the other end of the board, it had to be 'king-ed' by putting another checker of the same color on top of it. The other brother argued back that all he had to do was turn it over because on the flip side of each checker was a crown. If these brothers were anything like me and my brother Craig, they would have ended up wrestling until the little brother (me) started to cry and call for mommy.

---

[35] Author's paraphrase
[36] 2 Cor. 5:19-20

Did you know that most store-bought checkers these days have a crown on one side and a star on the other so that you can turn it into a king? I didn't know that until someone pointed it out and I started looking and sure enough those little black and red plastic disks do have a crown on one side. The company also makes the checkers with little ridges around the edge so you can securely place one checker on top of another to make it a king. I guess you can do it both ways!

Why does this bit of useless trivia matter? First, it might come up in a game of Trivial Pursuit and you'll have the answer and everyone will think you're brilliant! But more important, it helps us think about the letter L in the old Calvinistic acrostic, T.U.L.I.P. So far I've offered the church two new ways to highlight our Christian faith for a 21st century audience: **T- Triune Love**: experiencing God's love as it is shown to us through the Creator, Redeemer and Spirit. It's a love that is available to everyone on earth. The **U- Unlimited Election**: can mean that we are chosen or elected to be blessed by God before the foundations of the earth, so we can be a blessing to all others, the possibilities are unlimited! Now, I'm suggesting that the L stand for **Limitless Reconciliation**. Or another way of putting it is to say it's about a **70 x 7 attitude** of the soul.

Can you recall what Jesus was talking about when he said to Peter that forgiveness isn't limited to two or three chances, but 70 X 7 times[37] (an infinite number)? What does this mean to you?

---
[37] Matt. 18:21-22

I used to have a black and white picture hanging on my pastor's study wall. I think I tore it out of a magazine and framed it. It was just a bunch of straight lines, hundreds of them; 490 of them…over top of each other filling up the small canvas. Nothing else, just a bundle of short vertical lines. It was a conversation starter as parishioners saw it on the wall. "What's that?" they'd ask. I'd say, "Limitless Reconciliation". "Uh?" I'd explain, "That's how many times Jesus forgives us. You can't count how many times." They'd get it. I hope they still remember it and live like forgiven people.

In Reformation times, the 'L' stood for Limited Atonement, and it meant that the work of the cross of Jesus Christ was limited only for those who truly believed it to be for them and understood the cross's implications on faith and life and eternity. But by emphasizing the limited nature of salvation, it made many question what happens to all those in history, today and in the future who did not or will not know about Jesus and the gospel. Of course that created an effective missionary outreach starting in the 19th Century in which the Presbyterian denomination was on the cutting edge. The Presbyterians were the first denomination to have a National Missions Board, but even with our best efforts, many around the world die without hearing a sincere presentation of the gospel. What happens to them and what happened to those who lived *before* Jesus' day? These questions remain impossible to answer even by the greatest theologians.

Such questions come when we emphasize the limits of the gospel. But what happens when we emphasize what is unlimited in the gospel? Can it catch the ear of the many spiritually open people who think the church is only concerned about who's going to hell and who's not? Caring about the lost is paramount, but can we share the unlimited nature of the gospel with our neighbors and coworkers and dorm-mates in hopes that they might find in our church a place where they can sense the limitless grace and genuine, triune love of God for them?

Have you ever wondered what happens to the souls of those who lived before Jesus' time or those who have never heard an effective presentation of the gospel? How have you reconciled this with the God of love expressed in Jesus' preaching and teaching? Have you ever heard a satisfactory sermon on this? If so, how was it explained? Do you agree with that interpretation? Jot down your thoughts on this and ponder them today.

Prayer: O Lord of all life and breath: I know you are Creator, Redeemer and Spirit and the only true God. But I often wonder about the things that puzzle our human minds and find hard to understand. Help my understanding and where understanding fails, let my faith sustain me. I pray for all who still have yet to hear the effective message of the gospel and trust that they will discover your love and grace. Amen.

Notes:

Chapter Ten

Read Psalm 136:1-15

What comes in unlimited quantities in the gospel? **Reconciliation.** The Apostle Paul said it best to the Corinthian Church some 2000 years ago; *"When anyone is joined to Christ, she or he is a new creation; the old is gone, and the new has come. All this is done by God, who through Christ changed us from enemies into God's friends and gave us the task of making others God's friends as well."* (II Cor. 5: 17-18) This is reconciliation language. Paul goes on to say that the task we have been given is to share with as many as possible that God is trying to make everyone God's friends by not keeping an account of our sin but offering a fresh start. And then Paul says, "We beg you, let God change you."
(II Cor. 5:19-20)

This brings me back to the checker piece that is marked with a star and a crown. Like a coin, it has two sides. On one side of Limitless Reconciliation is the never-ending love of God for the world. That's our message, that's what the church has to tell the world. *God loves you and wants to be in relationship with all people.* Paul even pleads with the church… tell as many people as possible that God wants to be their friend!

Like the checker piece, there is another side to Limitless Reconciliation. Brian McLaren, in A Generous Orthodoxy says that instead of speculating on the scope of Limited Atonement, a kindler, gentler Calvinism could concentrate on what is unlimited in the gospel: reconciliation. But it's not just God being willing to reconcile and heal broken relationships with sinners like us, it's also those who have had their relationship with God healed, are called to be healers of relationships in the world. This means that we're always to pray to be forgiven by God as we forgive others, always love God and neighbor, and never ask the question, "Who is my neighbor?" in order to avoid limiting the scope of our love and care. Because God comes to us in Christ (Emmanuel), as the Neighbor to all, it moves us to become peace ambassadors of Christ to all.[38] Paul says we are ambassadors for God. We represent the gospel in our lives.

The flip side of the checker piece is just as important as the other side. A coin would have no value unless it had a head and a tail. Limitless Reconciliation is a two-sided doctrine that people today yearn to know and understand so they can enjoy a full and gracious life. Just as God reconciles us to God-self, we offer ourselves as reconcilers in a world that is filled with conflict, division, strife, and discord. Maybe when someone sees how we act, they may better understand how God acts.

God loves us and wants to heal the broken relationship between God and humanity. The Lord does that through the cross of Christ. Now God wants those new friends to not only tell others about the good news, but act it out in their own lives.... even if reconciliation means forgiving 70x7 times as Jesus advised his friend Simon Peter. [39]

---

[38] A Generous Orthodoxy, Pg. 196
[39] Matt. 18:21-22

I think those, like me, who are Presbyterian will particularly resonate with this text. You see, the Greek word Paul uses for 'ambassadors' for Christ, (or as the Good News Bible has it, 'friendmakers' for God which describes our task in reconciliation,) is the same word that gives name to the denomination; *"Presbeuomen"* or Presbyterians.

But this is not limited to Presbyterians, or should I say we are all presbyterians (with a small p). We are all called to live out our faith as a calling in which God has established before the foundations of the earth and we take on the humble task of being friendmakers for God in word and deed. This kind of calling requires faith, humility, courage and strength of spirit. At the table of the Lord, in worship, study, service and fellowship, we find all we need to be 'presbyterians', ambassadors, and friendmakers for God no matter what name is on the front sign of the church we attend.

What in the world is a 'friendmaker for God"? What would that look like in your life? Take a few minutes to consider this.

What comes in unlimited quantities in the gospel? **Reconciliation.** Instead of speculating on the scope of Limited Atonement, a kindler, gentler Calvinism would concentrate on what is unlimited in the gospel: **reconciliation.** But it's not just God being willing to reconcile and heal broken relationships with sinners like us, it's also those who have had their relationship with God healed and are now called to be healers of relationships in the world. We are wounded healers, a term Catholic priest and writer Henri Nouwen coined so many years ago. Paul could have said we are *repatriated ambassadors*.

God loves us and wants to heal the broken relationship between God and humanity. The Lord does that through the cross of Christ. Now God wants those new friends not only to tell others about the good news, but also act it out in their own lives. By virtue of just being a faithful disciple of any denomination or church, we live out the calling in which God pre destined before the foundations of the earth; the humble task of being friendmakers for God in word and deed. Paul wasn't writing to just one particular denomination who happens to be named for that Greek word he used in II Corinthians, he was writing to all who have a saving knowledge of Jesus Christ.

Prayer: Let me find the love and courage to live out Limitless Reconciliation in my daily life and let my lifestyle demonstrate such limitless hope for the world. Amen.

Notes:

Chapter Eleven

Read Ephesians 2:11-19

I

Inspiring Grace. Pay it forward is another way of saying, *Inspiring Grace*. In Catherine Ryan Hyde's novel <u>Pay It Forward</u> that was later a hit movie, Trevor McKinney and his classmates are challenged by their social studies teacher to change the world. Written on the blackboard the challenge reads:

"Think of an idea to change our world – and put it into action."

Trevor is mesmerized by the possibility that he might be able to change the world. As Trevor bikes home where he and his alcoholic mother live, he detours to a place where the homeless gather. An unkempt, unshaven man catches Trevor's attention. Motivated by the challenge, he invites the man to sleep in his garage. Trevor's mother is unaware of this arrangement and happens on him in the garage working on a broken down pickup. Startled, she holds him at gunpoint, and asks him to explain himself. He starts the truck to prove he was doing what he said he was doing and tells her about her son's kindness. He says, "Somebody comes along like your son and gives me a leg up, I'll take it. I can't mess up again, or I'll be dead. I'm just paying it forward." Confused, she asks, "What's paying it forward?"

Trevor explains to his class his amazing plan of paying it forward. To explain it, Trevor draws a circle on the blackboard and says, "That's me." Underneath, he draws three other circles, saying, "That's three other people. I'm going to help them, but it has to be something really big- something they can't do for themselves. So I do it for them, and they do it for three people. That's nine people." And nine lives turn into 27. "Paying it forward" changes the lives of the rich, the poor, the homeless, and even a prisoner.[40] It changes Trevor's life and his teacher's and his mom's, as well.

Pay it forward is another way of saying the "I" of our new T.U.L.I.P, *Inspiring Grace*. Can you think of a way that you can pay it forward? You've been blessed in spades, how have you found ways to pass on the grace of God? Paying it forward is another way of saying, *Inspiring Grace*; the I in the new version of the old Calvinistic acrostic, T.U.L.I.P.

In Reformation times and the centuries that followed, the I….meant that God's grace was at work in believers even before they knew they needed it. The Methodists call it prevenient grace. God's grace was the cause of one's salvation and the end result of it. It cannot be resisted and it cannot be stopped. This was good news at a time when the church

---

[40] Movie Based Illustrations, by C Larson and A. Zahn. 2003 Zondervan, Grand Rapids, MI Pg. 118

doctrine of the day said that one's salvation depended on how *good* someone acted or *how much* was sacrificed or donated to the Church. In fact, the church of the day was selling certificates of salvation. Even peasants, if they could scrape together the money, could buy a church-issued certificate (an indulgence) for himself or herself or a loved one that guaranteed entrance into heaven or ease in purgatory. In other words, salvation depended on one's own efforts.

Luther and Calvin came along with a corrective message, saying that it is not by works, but by grace alone through faith that we are made right with God.[41] And the grace of God is active and instigating our salvation. The corrective was so divisive that it split the European church in two. And even today, Protestants and Catholics differ markedly on the role of good works in salvation. But over time, some came to understand the doctrine of irresistible grace as some kind of dominating, deterministic force that in a mechanistic and unstoppable progression of events, swept the believer along in a wave of uncontrollable destiny. Like it or not, you were going to be a Christian, even if you came kicking and screaming. Looking at grace this way, you can see why even Protestants often argue about this oft-debated doctrine.

On the other hand, all Christians, no matter what brand name is on the front sign, acknowledge that grace plays a leading role in salvation somewhere along the line. For Methodists who historically believed in 'free will' when it comes to salvation, still hold to the role prevenient grace plays. It's

---

[41] See Ephesians 2:9

grace working behind the scenes readying a soul for salvation. And if that's the case, then maybe we can begin to talk about grace in a way that we all can agree upon. One thought from theologian Brian McLaren is:

"Rather than picturing God's grace as a dominating, almost mechanistic force that cannot be resisted, a kinder, gentler, gospel for the 21st Century would view God's grace as a passionate, powerful, personal desire of the Triune God to shower the church with healing and joy and every good thing. And having received this grace freely and fully, the church would then be inspired by grace to freely and fully extend that grace to others in an overflow of good works and acts of kindness and mercy, yielding a truly generous orthodoxy." [42]

Can you image a church full of people who pull out of the parking lot every Sunday after services overflowing with Christian acts of kindness and good works? Even more, as Jesus puts it, blessings in good measure, pressed down, shaken together, running over, and filling your lap so much, you're inspired to give it away. [43]

An old Celtic tale tells about the time King Oswald of Northumbria (Britain) had heard about the blessings of the Christian gospel and sent a messenger to the bishop, asking

---

[42] A Generous Orthodoxy, pg. 196
[43] Luke 6:38

that he send a teacher from the Iona Community to his kingdom. The monk soon returned complaining that the people of Northumbria were brutes, barbarous and too obstinate to hear the gospel. One monk, named Aidan, said that it was unfair to judge the people like that. He suggested they follow the apostles', who began by giving the people the milk of the gospel, gradually nourishing them until they were capable of digesting spiritual meat. All were impressed and sent Aidan to the court of King Oswald. (That's what happens when you make a suggestion at a meeting. They give you the job.)

The King was impressed with Aidan and offered him an island to build a church. At low tide, the King could walk from his castle to the church on dry ground. The people of Northumbria slowly accepted the gospel. Many of the wealthy offered Aidan gifts, but he did not keep them. Instead he passed them on to the poor and needy, as well as ransoming slaves.

The old Celtic tale goes on that on Easter Sunday, King Oswald invited Aidan to a lavish holiday meal served on the castle's finest silver dishes. As Aidan lifted his hands to bless the meal, a servant rushed into the hall and announced that a mob of hungry peasants was at the gate asking for charity and something to eat on Easter. The King instantly gathered the holiday meal and gave it away. Then he took the silver dishes and smashed them, giving out pieces of silver to the needy people of his kingdom. Aidan was so impressed with the King's act of kindness, that he took the King's hands and blessed him. [44] Can you see inspiring grace at work, here? If there is a moral to this ancient tale it must be that acts of kindness and mercy gush from a grace-filled soul. How have you seen inspiring grace at work today?

In the book <u>Conspiracy of Kindness</u>, Steve Sjogren (Showgren) tells the true story of Joe Delaney and his 8-year-old son, Jared. Having a catch in the back yard, Jared asked, "Dad, is there a God?" Joe, who had only went to church a few times as a boy, said, "I don't know."

Jared raced into the house and came out with a balloon on a string, a pen, and a 3x5 card. He wrote a note on the card: Dear God, if you are real and you are there, send people you know to my dad and me." He tied the card to the string and let it float away. Joe prayed, "God, I hope you're watching."

Two days later Joe and Jared pulled into a car wash sponsored by Sjogren's church and when they went to pay, Steve said it was on the house. It was a way to be of service to the community, no strings attached. "Are you guys Christians, the kind who believe in God?" Joe asked out the window. "Yes, we're that kind of Christians," Sjogren said. From that encounter, Joe and Jared got acquainted with Jesus Christ. Many people may be only one act of Christian kindness away from experiencing a boatload of blessings of God.[45] I believe God is saying to the church today, pay it forward; exhibit inspiring grace. Inspiring Grace is God's

---

[44] Celtic Parables, R. Van De Weyer, 1998 Northstone Pub. Inc. pg. 27-8
[45] Conspiracy of Kindness, Regal Books, 2008

passionate, powerful and personal desire to shower the beloved with healing and joy and every good thing. Let the inspiring grace that God has given you in good measure, pressed down, shaken together, and running over, inspire you to freely and fully give it away. Pay it forward!

Has 'pay it forward' been something you've ever done? If so, how?

Prayer: Lord of all life and love, let me keep my ears open to ways that I may help others in your name. When I hear of a far away disaster on the news, I'll pray and even give a donation to help. When I hear of a neighbor in need, I will offer to lend a hand. When I know of a concern that needs quiet counsel, I'll offer it in love. Amen.

Notes:

Chapter Twelve

Read Psalm 136

T.U.L.I.P- A Kinder, Gentler Calvinism for the 21st Century: Passionate, Persistent Saints.

It is a mouthful but maybe it has to be, seeing it's a new challenge to the established church to consider new ways of expressing the gospel in our day and age. The original T.U.L.I.P. was an easy way to remember the basics of our Reformed theology that addressed the issues and spiritual questions of 16th Century Europe.

Over the centuries, these doctrines have been disputed by other denominations, been contrasted with more current theologies, and even today Presbyterians argue amongst themselves about them. A brief review of the classical mode may be in order. Can you, in your own words give a brief definition of each letter we've looked at so far using our newer definitions?

T.

U.

L.

I.

A review of the traditional T.U.L.I.P. follows:

T- Total Depravity - human beings are totally corrupted by sin and can do nothing to cause their own salvation. A kinder, gentler way of understanding the gospel might be to say the *T- Triune Love: All people can and need to experience God's love as it is shown through the Trinity: Creator, Redeemer and Spiritual Presence of God.*

U- Unconditional Election - God chose or elected a people before the foundations of the earth to carry out his purposes. You and I being Christian, God's people, isn't about how good or faithful we are; God chose us for service even before we were born and not by our choice nor because of our good efforts! A kinder, gentler expression of faith that may get more people to consider being a Christian is to say the *U- Unselfish Election, meaning that God blessed his people so that his people then could bless all others. What we have, we share in Jesus' name.*

L- Limited Atonement - taught the church that Jesus' death on the cross was effective for those who accept it and understand it. Only those who can accept the gift of salvation receive it. A kinder, gentler way of expressing the work of the cross may be to say the *L- Limitless Reconciliation. God offers reconciliation to us and then we are to offer reconciliation to others. God makes us his friends and we are called to be friendmakers for God and to befriend our neighbors for Jesus' sake.*

I. **Irresistible Grace** means our salvation, from beginning to end, is the work of God's grace, not our own doing. Like clay in the hands of a potter, God molds us into his people. The clay conforms to the irresistible workings of the potter. God molds us into disciples. Some would say whether we like it or not. A kinder, gentler way of talking about grace may be to call it, *I- Inspiring Grace. God passionately showers grace on us that makes us want to shower Christian acts of kindness and mercy upon others.*

This brings us to the last letter of the acrostic T.U.L.I.**P**.

Perseverance of the Saints was how it traditionally is expressed. The classical meaning is that no matter what happens, what the circumstances, those who are called by God and are in the church will see it through. God, who began a good work in you, will see it through to the end. God never takes back his gift of salvation even if we turn our backs on God from time to time. The hope we have, as Christians, cannot be dashed.[46] "Nothing can separate us from God in Christ Jesus our Lord" is how the Apostle Paul says it. "For God does not change his mind about whom God chooses and blesses." (Rom. 11:29)

Yes, saints will see it through to the end and on into glory.... Like the saints who've gone before us... just knowing this promise gives us hope, but maybe we can put it another way. Instead of saying we just *endure* life, what if our message was that we could be living life as if it's a thrill ride, a grand adventure.

---

[46] Rom. 5:2

Life with Christ is an exciting adventure, or at least it should be. Like Pilgrim in Bunyan's Pilgrim's Progress, or Tolkien's Bilbo Baggins, or like Peter, Susan, Edmond and Lucy stepping through the wardrobe into C.S. Lewis' Narnia, our adventure began at baptism and we're headed for eternity with God. What a difference the adventure would be if we said the journey would be made by **P- Passionate, persistent saints.**

> "Nothing can separate us from God

Saints? What are saints? Who are saints? Are we supposed to wear halos? What store sells them and do they come in my size? Can I order mine on Amazon? Look around and see if you can find anyone with a halo.

According to the Bible Dictionary, biblical saints are 'people who have been set apart and consecrated to worship and be in service to God'.[47] Saints are believers, they're you and me and all who are God's people. And yes saints can still act like sinners from time to time, even jerks, yet in God's eyes, we're still saints. Passionate, persistent saints will make a difference in the world.

---

[47] The Dictionary: Finding meaning in God's Word. 2001 Nelson Pub. Pg. 332

McLaren says, "*Saints could be unflagging in their attempts to live and share the gospel, resilient after failure, persevering in adversity, persistent over centuries and across generations. We could have an unquenchable hope, confident that God will never fail to fulfill a promise, and be passionate to join God in expressing saving love for our world until every promise comes true.*" [48]

This quote makes me think of question #60 in the Belonging to God catechism Presbyterians use to teach the faith to children. It's the last question and answer in the catechism and it concludes a section on the Lord's Prayer. It goes like this: *Q: Why does the prayer end with 'amen'? A: "Amen" means 'so be it' or 'let it be so'. It expresses our complete confidence in God, who makes no promise that will not be kept and whose love endures forever.* [49] The saints of God are 'amen' people. By God's Spirit, our lives line up with God's will for our lives and that's a firm promise and a sure hope.

"In Hebrew, 'amen' means 'firm' or 'reliable'. In NT Greek, it means 'truly' or 'surely'. In English it basically means 'true' or 'Yes, it is true'. According to its many uses in the Bible, 'amen' can be a stamp of approval…confirm a contract….and it's another way of saying "Thus says the Lord". Jesus said it often; 'Surely, surely (truly, truly) I say to you…"[50] And what does Jesus say to the church? Be passionate. Be persistent. Be the kind of people who know

---

[48] A Generous Orthodoxy. Pg. 197
[49] Belonging to God: A First Catechism PCUSA Louisville, KY
[50] Meditations on Belonging to God: A First Catechism, Keith M. Curran, Witherspoon Press. Louisville, KY 2005

that they are the family of God; God's people who have a purpose and destiny. We can and will change the world for Christ's sake.

The kind of saints I'm talking about go after life. I remember a Saturday when the church youth group from First Presbyterian Church of New Castle, PA went to Kennywood Amusement Park in Pittsburgh. The line for the bumper cars was long and it gave us time to watch others on the metal rink. Riders ran to the little cars, strapped themselves in and when the buzzer sounded, drove in direct contradiction to the name of the ride. They maneuvered the strange little cars around the rink as if their insurance rates were at stake. I watched as teens, grandmas, a guy in a turban and a dozen others avoided any altercation and when they were hit, acted insulted, yet they seemed to be having fun.

Then there was the minority who stepped on the gas as if the buzzer was the green flag at a NASCAR race and aimed for the nearest car. Bam! Bam! Again and again, they slammed into any car they could find. Broad grins arched across each face and laughter erupted when they got bumped. For two whole minutes, they had a blast!

I want us to be bumper car saints! Go after life. Life is specially made for people to go after it with all their might and heart and soul! It seems like most people only take a cautious ride around the rink of life, enjoying the smooth and uninterrupted times and being upset when the bumps in life hit us. But haven't you noticed that the saints who really enjoy life, who really live as if life is a thrill ride and they are the luckiest kids on the block because they have a season pass to the park.... haven't you noticed that these saints, bumper car saints, are the people we envy and these are the saints who have a joy, joy, joy, joy down in their hearts? They seem to be the people who get things done, too.

When was the last time you rode the bumper cars? How did you approach the ride? For you, were they the dodgem cars or were they the bumper cars?

St. Paul helps us understand the attitude we should be working on as saints of God:

Now that we have been reconciled with God, we have peace in Jesus Christ. He's chosen us for this life and inspired us with God's grace. We can even celebrate where we are along life's journey; and shout with praise even when we're hemmed in with troubles, because we know how troubles can develop passionate patience in us, and how that patience in turn forges the tempered steel of virtue, keeping us alert for whatever God will do next. And this promise doesn't disappoint because God's poured out his Triune Love into our hearts and we know his Presence. [51] (Rom. 5:1-5)

Maybe what we can do as a church is offer a kinder, gentler way of expressing our historic Faith. Those who have closed themselves off to the traditional gospel message might hear a new song that resonates in their souls at a church that

---

[51] Scripture taken from *The Message*. Copyright 1993, 1994, 1995, 1996, 2000, 2001, 2002. Used by permission of NavPress Publishing Group.

embraces a new TULIP for the 21st Century. Can you picture those who think church is quietly sitting in a pew, dressed up and just listening to a message from the 1950's era? Surprisingly, there are loads of folks who think that's what church is like. I know they're mistaken, but can we put ourselves in their shoes? Can we think of ways we might express our faith, Christian service, and worship in a way that gets their attention without selling out to culture? That's my hope for the church today.

Saints of God, sing 'Alleluia!' Saints of God, soar with passion and persistence because the adventure of a lifetime is only getting started. We are the passionate, persistent saints of God. Don't just endure- blossom, flourish, shine, rise up on eagle's wings and soar. Amen and amen.

Notes:

Chapter Thirteen

Read Lev. 19:15-18

"Can we see God's image in those who do not look like our reflection in the mirror?" so asked a rabbi. As saints of God, one of the main objectives of the church today is to find ways to reach out to those who have closed themselves off from the good news of Jesus Christ. Often, because of how the established church has hurt or sidelined or offended or excluded people, our neighbors don't even think of going to church as a viable option for them. What our neighbors remember from childhood about the church or the stereotypes they glean from the media about Christians, sound so old fashioned to them.

 The church I serve and our grace-oriented theology often is a surprising and refreshing shock to those who attend after being away from church for a long time. I hear it almost every week from visitors or in our phone conversations as I follow up on those who attend worship and sign our guest register. Their pleasant surprise gives me joy as I see this positive response to a new Calvinism for the 21st Century. Can you put yourself in their shoes? What do you think they see and hear and feel in worship at a church that surprises them? What do you think turned them off to the church in the past? Jot down a

few of your thoughts and look around this Sunday in worship for someone new and introduce yourself to them. Make them feel welcome.

Prayer: Lord of the pilgrim and the stranger. Remind us that one time we were strangers at church once. What must it be like for newcomers at our church, O Lord? What can I do to make them feel welcome and wanted? O Lord, let me walk a mile in their shoes so that they may want to walk with you in life. Amen.

Notes:

Read Isaiah 51:1-3

One of the keys to being persistent saints is knowing that, no matter what, God will be with us. That assurance is expressed in Isaiah 51:1-3 as you have read. Isaiah is also the one who predicted that God would come into the world as Immanuel, God with us. In Matthew 1:23 we find that prophesy fulfilled in the one who came into the world in Bethlehem. [Look up Matthew 1:23 and read this wonderful promise.]

This is the same God who walked with our primordial parents in the Garden and went ahead of the Hebrews as a beacon through the desert. In the New Testament God's presence is known to us as the Holy Spirit who lives in each believer as the sustaining God who sees us through. The same promise is lifted up when we speak the 23rd Psalm. God is seeing us through even the darkest moments in life, holding our hand as we walk through the valley of the shadows.

During the fateful events of Jesus last days, what must the first disciples have thought as the week moved from exuberant celebration to dark Good Friday? Do you think they had a sense of God's constant presence even in those dark moments? And what about you? In your dark moments, do you sense that God is with you? The promise of the P. of our new TULIP is that God will see us through, which in turn, gives us the faith, courage and spiritual stamina to be persistent, passionate saints.

Prayer: *Lord of the dark moments; see us through our Gethsemanes and cross moments so that we may walk through and come out the other side of the dark valley, out of the shadows and into the light once again. We trust this in Christ who will see us through. Amen.*

Notes:

Read Rev. 3:20

When we talk about passion, what does that mean to you? The Church calls the week between Palm Sunday and Easter, Passion Week. Mel Gibson's film, *The Passion*, chronicles these last days of Jesus' life. Many questioned Gibson's portrayal and theology, but the gut-wrenching, tear-stained experience of seeing the movie cannot be ignored. Why? Passion has multiple meanings. There's pathos, pain, feelings, excitement, emotion, unquenched dedication, love, sacrifice, total commitment, to name just a few synonyms. And all these elements enter into the story of Passion Week. It's filled with raw, often uncontrollable emotion. It's also driven by a love that is total and dedicated to the goal of one life for many.

As passionate saints, is there anything we're that excited about, dedicated to, or emotionally charged about? A kinder, gentler Calvinism offers a vast array of options for the contemporary church. One of them highlighted at the church I served is our ministry of **hospitality and welcome.** It's the one constant we heard from new members and it's the reason the church has a strong, consistent growth pattern for the last decade plus. As our congregation has grown from 235 members ten years ago to over 540 at the time of this writing, the one comment heard over and over again is the wonderful, grace filled welcome our visitors and new members receive. What a nice complement! In fact, it's the #1 reason visitors return for a second time. Being friendly isn't something we can say about ourselves. All churches claim to be friendly, whether it is true or not. This is something that someone else has to say about the church. But when you hear it time and time again as the reason people join the church and get involved with Christ's people, then that's something to acknowledge with a prayer of thanksgiving.

St. Paul advises us to take on the same attitude of Christ in our daily walk and reading today's text offers us the chance to follow suit. The welcome the Risen Lord is hoping to receive is like the welcome our church neighbors are hoping to receive when they attend worship. Christ is standing at the door, hoping to be invited in. Once inside, he'll break bread (become a friend) to us. I think that's what the church's neighbors are hoping for, too.

This Sunday, will you seek out a visitor or newcomer and welcome them to church. Maybe you'll notice someone who hasn't been in a while and they seem a while. Between hand shakes with your friends, save a moment and a prayer for someone you have not seen around before. Such an intentional effort is being Christ-like, remembering that Christ is standing at the door, hoping for an invitation to come in and become friends.

Prayer: Can I be like you, O Risen Christ? Can I see you in one of the least of these? Can I remember that I was a stranger once and appreciated a warm welcome? Can I find a passion to be a "friendmaker for God" this Sunday? With your help I can. Amen.

Notes:

Read John 7:37-38

Emergent Church theologian, Brian McLaren says, "*Saints could be unflagging in their attempts to live and share the gospel, resilient after failure, persevering in adversity, persistent over centuries and across generations. We could have an unquenchable hope, confident that God will never fail to fulfill a promise, and be passionate to join God in expressing saving love for our world until every promise comes true.*"[52]

This is a great way to think about being passionate, persistent saints. Today, maybe you can take a moment to list a few ways you could put this vision into action this week. See if you can find 4 ways to be a passionate, persistent saint of God.

1.

2.

3.

4.

---

[52] A Generous Orthodoxy. Pg. 197

Prayer: Let your Spirit flow through my mind where new thoughts can emerge. Let your Spirit beat with my heart so I may be in sync with you. Let your Spirit capture my imagination so I can find ways to be a passionate and persistent saint. Amen.

Notes:

Read I Cor. 13:4-7

Passionate saints are also imperfect people. No one has the market on the whole truth. No one fits God's plan perfectly. No one comes to God unblemished. No one gets the prize for being perfect. Scripture says only one person fits that bill and it was Jesus. No one else, especially not me, and you are likely saying the same thing about yourself right now.

> # No Perfect People Allowed!

In St. Paul's love poem, we find the essence relationship among imperfect saints. Here is your assignment for the day. Write out this famous text using your own words. I've included it below in the old King James Version that many will easily recognize. Paraphrase them for your life today. Maybe you can write it out using terminology from work or the home, family or friendship. You be the creative force today and come up with a personal version of this famous text on love. Then, read it over throughout the day. Tape it to the desk, dashboard or fridge. Let it be your prayer today.

I Cor. 13: 4 Charity suffereth long, and is kind; charity envieth not; charity vaunteth not itself, is not puffed up, 5 Doth not behave itself unseemly, seeketh not her own, is not easily provoked, thinketh no evil; **6** *Rejoiceth not in iniquity, but rejoiceth in the truth;* **7** *Beareth all things, believeth all things, hopeth all things, endureth all things. (KJV)*

Your Version:

Read Luke 19:28-40

We've come far. Some have learned about the traditional Reformed key points of our Presbyterian tradition for the first time. Others have been reminded of truths learned long ago. Then we ventured into new territory, seeing if the church can speak to upcoming generations with the same truth but in an updated, kinder, gentler fashion suited for 21st Century Christians. It has added another handful of arrows to our quiver as we engage a cynical culture desperate to hear good news of some kind, yet reluctant to consider the Good News of Christ. Now, we're better equipped to speak the truth in love as St. Paul instructs us to do. Is there someone in your life who yearns for good news but has been turned off from old-fashioned sounding religious claims?

I think we all know someone like that. Their list of complaints about the church or God is long. But now we have some new thoughts to share and inviting promises to offer. The new T.U.L.I.P. for the 21st Century may be just the thing they're looking for.

T.U.L.I.P.

-Triune Love
-Unselfish Election
-Limitless Reconciliation
-Inspiring Grace
-Passionate, Persistent Saints of God, called the Church.

Think of that one person today and say a prayer that the grace of God will begin to heal the wounds of the past and that somehow, God might lead you to a moment or opportunity when you can share the good news with him or her. You now are equipped with the gospel that connects with 21st Century people. And, who knows what God can do through you!

I can do all things in Christ who strengthens me.

Write the name here:

_____

Prayer: *As we end this chapter, let me be ready to put into practice what I've learned so that others may find a godly shalom in my testimony. Amen.*

Notes:

Putting a New T.U.L.I.P. to Work

Read John 13:1-9

Maybe what we need today, more than anything else is to be a church that offers a kinder, gentler way of expressing the Faith:
- where we believe God's Triune love is for everyone,
- where unselfish election motivates the elect to be a blessing to all others,
- where limitless reconciliation calls us to be friendmakers for God,
- how inspiring grace challenges us to pay it forward,
- and where passionate, persistent saints savor every ounce of life.

Saints of God, say, 'Alleluia'!

And we now have a new T.U.L.I.P. to inspire those who have closed themselves off from the traditional gospel message and a creative way of sharing a refreshing word, a new song that may resonate in their souls. Saints of God, say 'Alleluia! The Lord has given us a new song.' Saints of God, soar with passion and persistence because the adventure of a lifetime, the 21st Century, is just getting started.

Prayer: To God alone be the glory. Amen.

Notes:

My Notes and reflections…